# I WILL OVERCOME

---

*A Story of Love, Hope*
*& Forgiveness*

---

*Tommy Don Talley Jr.*

Cover Design: Janie Lott

Interior Design: Janie Lott

Published by: Tommy Talley

I Will Overcome: A Story of Love, Hope, & Forgiveness. Tommy Don Talley, Jr. First Edition.

ISBN: 978-1-6664-0031-1

# DEDICATION

*This book is dedicated to the woman who taught me to love, mi vida, Karla. You've been in my life for more than a decade, and you still surprise me every day with how loving, courageous, and strong you are. You are beautiful inside and out, and I couldn't imagine a day without you by my side. Thank you for being the backbone of our family. I am sorry for all that I have put this family through, I know I am not perfect, not even close. But daily I am trying to be better, not just for me, but for all of us. This book might shed some light on a few things you may not know about me and why this battle has been so hard for me. I hope that after reading this you will gain some more hope, love, and forgiveness, as I have. I love you more than words can describe.*

*This book is also dedicated to my beautiful children:, Annabelle, Aiden, and Emiliano. You are the reason I keep pushing every day to be a better version of myself. It's all for you.*

*No matter what obstacles you face in life, I hope you remember that nothing can keep you from being the very best version of you. We can forgive, grow, and learn. Our past doesn't have to dictate our lives, but we can use it to shape us in positive ways, even when we have had negative experiences.*

*May God continue to keep you safe, happy, and healthy every day. Mommy and Daddy love you more than anything in this world.*

*This book is also dedicated to kids in situations like the one I lived through, whether they are dealing with abuse, addiction, trauma, or facing starvation or homelessness. You have the power to take what life has given you and make it beautiful. I urge you to choose to break free from what holds you back. Choose Love, Hope, and Forgiveness. With that choice comes a new life—a life filled with clarity, intention, and happiness.*

# TABLE OF CONTENTS

# INTRODUCTION

**M**y reality as a child was constant isolation and having no one to depend on but myself. Very early on in my childhood, I realized I had no other choice but to be strong and self-reliant. After my two younger sisters were born, it wasn't just me I had to be strong for, but also them. This wasn't the traditional sort of strength you want to extend to your siblings—it was more intense, almost desperate, because I wanted to protect them and keep them safe. Somewhere in my innocent mind, I thought I could save all of us.

My parents had a lot on their plate, and it was very noticeable to my sisters and I. My parents were deep into their addictions to drugs and alcohol. They also battled mental illness and were preoccupied all of the time. There was no space in their lives for us. They didn't have the capacity to care for themselves, let alone three children. When we were left alone, we would use our imaginations to keep us entertained. We'd play games like tag and hide and seek, and we'd make pillow forts with the sofa cushions. There was a game we played a lot called "house." In this game we would pretend to be something we were not—a happy family. My oldest sister, Tiffany, and I were usually the mom and dad, and our younger sister Emily was our baby.

We would pretend to do all kinds of normal household activities, like cleaning the house, cooking dinner, and going to the store. Emily would pretend to be hungry, and we'd feed her. She'd pretend to be sleepy, and we'd lay her in bed, tuck her in, and put her to sleep. Emily would pretend to be sad or hurt, and here came Mommy and Daddy (Tiffany and I) to comfort her. It's crazy how kids have such a capacity to give love and comfort, even amid chaos. Here we were, children suffering from severe verbal and physical abuse, oftentimes left alone, playing a happy family. In reality, we didn't receive much comfort in times of distress from our parents. Luckily, we had each other.

Growing up, I thought that people could tell I came from a broken home. I felt like no matter where I was, all eyes were on me. It was like people could tell we were struggling and we were scared, anxious, and sad. I would ask myself things like, "why me?" or "why us?" I thought the hardships we endured were isolated issues and were only happening to my siblings and I, and that every other household was like those on TV, where the parents were always so happy to be around each other and loved, cheered for, cared for, and nurtured their children. I yearned for that life with all of my heart. It wasn't until I grew older that I realized my idea of what a "normal" household looked like was far from accurate.

I realized that households like mine are actually quite common—much more common than they should be. I'm writing this book exactly for that reason: to help bring more awareness to what growing up in households like the one I was raised in was like. To show its effects, both short and long term. To show the children, young adults, and grown adults who have a story similar to mine that we are not alone. That we are loved, we are worthy, and there is a way out of the darkness.

I want kids in bad situations to know there is hope and healing ahead. I want to inspire them to have the courage to push through and be their best selves. Just like the way diamonds are formed under pressure, these kids can emerge from their experiences more beautiful and stronger than before.

I am also writing this book in hopes of breaking harmful family cycles. My experience has shown me how unaware people are of their actions and how those actions affect others. Despite all the things my parents put my sisters and me through, I don't think they truly understood the damage they were inflicting upon us. I want to raise awareness about additction, child abuse, and the lack of support for struggling children. We all have people around us that are struggling, but how far do we go to help those people, especially those closest to us? People don't like to talk about what happens behind closed doors to break the cycles of generational disfunction. I have worked hard to break the cycle of abuse I experienced in my own family, and I know that others can do the same. I hope my story provides comfort to a child who feels isolated or unseen, gives a young adult courage to speak up and seek help, or offers strength to an adult who is finally ready to treat their childhood wounds.

Lastly, this book is about forgiveness. I feel like people don't forgive enough. We can choose to be weighed down by the harm that others have caused, we can hold grudges, or we can learn how to forgive. I want others to find the power and ability to forgive and let go of the past like I have. When we forgive, we heal. When we heal, we move forward. I deserve to move forward, and so do you.

As you'll read about in this book, my experiences almost destroyed me. I was stuck in my trauma, and I couldn't see a way out. I had to forgive. It wasn't easy, but after everything I went through, after the pain that others have caused me, I'm still able to love those who hurt me. I saw firsthand the horrible mistakes people can make, but I've also seen that they can change. I want to share my travels down the complicated and difficult road to forgiveness. Along the way, it's important to remember to forgive yourself too, even if others don't.

# PART I
*A Difficult Childhood*

# CHAPTER 1:
# THE TRAP

I used to wonder how different my life would be if I had grown up in a different house. I used to dream about having a rich family and being given everything I could ever want: tons of toys, indestructible bikes, a gigantic swimming pool, the best clothes, and a perfect, happy family that did everything together. A life where there was lots of love, a feeling of safety and security, and a mother and father who were dedicated to their children. Maybe I was watching too much television.

The truth is, my family was far from ideal. I would see other families around me and on TV, and wonder why my life wasn't more like theirs. They seemed so normal and happy. When we would drive by parks around town, I would see families laughing together, having picnics, playing games, or playing with their dogs. I wondered what that felt like. There were many times I would feel a pit in my stomach and a lump in my throat because my life at home was so different from the lives those families seemed to have. I wanted that normalcy. More than that, I wanted to laugh and know what happiness felt like.

My life was a living nightmare, and I couldn't escape. "Fun" for my family meant not getting yelled at or hurt. "Fun" was just a rare break from the usual fear and tension. My sisters and I were always walking on eggshells, trying not to upset my irritable parents. Things as normal as playing too loudly, laughing, or dropping something could result in getting hit or screamed at, so we made every move in fear. We were all nervous children, and we never felt comfortable or safe. How could we? We would try to do things quietly and carefully. To others, we probably looked like careful and responsible kids, but inwardly, we were living in fear, always waiting for the next outburst or slap in the face.

I desperately wanted to wake up from my nightmare of a

life. I felt helpless and trapped. I didn't get the opportunities other children had. Not only did we not have the money, but my parents weren't interested in providing any opportunities for us. Besides, we didn't have time—every single day we were just trying to survive. My sisters and I were trying to survive abuse, and our parents were trying to survive their addictions.

Looking back at my early childhood, most of my memories are of traumatic events. Don't get me wrong: there were good days, but for some sad, strange reason, the bad days are the ones that stay with me and haunt me. I've had to learn how to deal with those memories, and maybe someday I'll remember more of the good stuff instead.

## Always on the Move

I've heard the story of August 11, 1993, the night I was born, about a million times. Rochelle, my father's cousin, tells me the story with a sparkle in her eyes. "The night your parents brought you home, you were wrapped in a big blanket," she said. "I uncovered your face, and you stared up at me with your big eyes. I melted. From that moment, I fell in love with you. I knew you were special."

As a newborn, I lived with my parents, my aunt, and my uncle in a house at 103rd and Avenue L on the southeast side of Chicago. Two years later, my sister Tiffany was born, and we moved to a house that my father's aunt owned in Calumet City. We moved again two years later, around the time that my sister Emily was born.

When my younger sisters entered the world, my family started moving around. Throughout my childhood, we moved all over Chicago and lived with many different family members.

Having to move around so much was hard on me. I was already a nervous and quiet kid, and every new environment brought even more uncertainties. I was constantly put into new schools with new classes and new teachers. With each new place and environment, I wondered if I would be safe.

During this time, any sudden movements or loud noises made me flinch. I startled easily, and I was always on the lookout for danger. Because I was so afraid, I seemed introverted to others.

Moving around a lot made me feel unstable. I wondered what was going to happen to me. Each new school and neighborhood that I was in felt scary and foreign. I was always an outsider, trying to figure out how to adjust to my new situation.

The last place my parents lived together was in Pilsen. My father was working as a traveling chef when we lived there, and I remember him going away for weeks at a time. It was around this time that my parents realized their marriage wasn't going to work and started the process of divorce.

Even when I was staying at one family member's place, I might be bounced around the next week to another. I could be with my mom or with Ray and Rochelle. I felt like I was stuck in the middle and had to pick a side. Both parties would say bad things about each other, and I would have to listen. I felt that I was expected to agree with what they were saying. I constantly felt guilty, like I was betraying the person I didn't side with. It was a lose-lose situation. Ray, Rochelle, my dad, and the rest of that side of the family would bash my mother constantly, and on the other side, my mom and her family would bash my father, Rochelle, and Ray. They would call each other foul names that should not be said around children. They would talk about each other's addictions, financial situations, living situations, physical looks, and poor choices. There was always name-calling when someone from the opposite party was mentioned. As a young boy, all I knew how to do was put my head down and stay quiet, hoping that one day the feud would end.

The worst part about being stuck in the middle was the fighting. I remember one specific incident when I was living on Avenue N with Ray and Rochelle, and my mom called to say she was coming to get me. Legally, Ray and Rochelle had to give me back to my mom, but because they didn't think that was the safest option for me, they were fighting as hard as they could to keep me.

Ray and Rochelle told me to hide in my room so that when my mom came, I wouldn't have to go with her. I remember feeling scared and nervous. I had a knot in my stomach. I felt nauseous and sweaty, and everything felt blurry. I wondered where I would end up. Would I have to go with my mom?

When my mom made these kinds of threats, she would often say she would be bringing her friends and family with her for backup. She would threaten to burn down or shoot up the house if Ray and Rochelle didn't turn me over. I felt scared for all of us.

I wasn't just worried about my mom taking me away from my home, but from my school, too. Ray and Rochelle used to tell me that if my mom showed up at the school, I had to tell the school staff that I didn't want to go with her. I remember days where I couldn't focus on schoolwork because I was worried that my mom would storm into the school and take me away. Every time the class intercom would sound, I vividly remember the feeling of my stomach dropping to my feet, my body tensing up, and my palms getting clammy. *Is this it? Is that the office calling to tell me my mom is here? Is this the day I need to make a decision about who I live with?* Both Ray and Rochelle and my mom wanted what was best for me, but what did I want? No one ever asked me, but if they had, I honestly wouldn't have known what to say. How could I make a decision, but more importantly, how could I live with the decision I made knowing that no matter my choice, someone would be hurt by it.

Thankfully, despite all the moving around, I was able to make friends easily, which made things a little easier to live with. I've always had an accepting and easygoing personality. Other children found me easy to get along with and wanted to hang out with me.

Even though I had friends, I liked it best when I was alone.

My experiences had taught me that people were unsafe to be around. When it was just me, I didn't have to worry about what other people were doing. I knew I wouldn't be scared by any loud noises or sudden movements. When I was alone, I could find a moment's peace, and that felt good. I wasn't antisocial, but it took me a while to figure out how to be comfortable around other people.

## Caring for My Sisters

Since I was the oldest sibling, I tried to comfort my sisters whenever I could despite the fact that I was also afraid. There were times when we would be stuck in the middle of the ridiculous fights between my parents, and my mother would use us as leverage against my father. Countless times, my mother would threaten to beat us if my father would not leave the house—sometimes she made even worse threats, such as putting pillows over our heads to smother us if he didn't leave. One day she actually made my siblings and I lay flat on the floor and threatened to put the pillows over our faces as we screamed and cried. Knowing that most times her threats were real, we complied with her demands. There I laid with my siblings on the floor telling them that things would be alright, trying to comfort them despite knowing this could be the moment our lives would end. I held my sisters' hands very tight on that floor, a symbol of a bond that would last a lifetime.

We felt my mother's hatred towards my father—we felt it in the blows to our bodies by the broomstick, her shoe, her hand, or whatever she had in arm's reach.

On the rare day that there weren't any arguments—usually days when one of my parents wasn't home—it was like a dream come true for my sisters and me.

I knew that my parents were physically stronger than my sisters and I, and I tried to protect them from getting hurt, especially by my mother. I knew that in order to avoid her abuse, we would have to behave. I tried to behave as best as I could and encouraged my sisters to do the same. My obedience was military-like. I knew what kinds of things could send my mother over the edge, and I helped my sisters avoid triggering her. We struggled together, and we always had each other's backs.

Eventually, everything blew up, and my parents split. My sisters and I were sent to live in separate places. I didn't see them too often, especially after they went back to live with my mom. There were many years where I only saw my sisters on holidays. We got along and there were never any issues between us, but it was difficult for me to maintain a relationship with them because of our living situations.

There is an ache and a loneliness that comes with being separated from your siblings. When you're little, you can't describe it, but you feel it. There were blocks of time when I knew I was safe, but I was worried my sisters weren't. I felt guilty. I missed them. I was torn between my own needs and my concern for them.

## My Parents

In the '90s, my parents weren't the most responsible people—actually, they weren't responsible at all. When I was a child, they were too preoccupied to care about taking care of some basic things in their life. This included their children.

I think everyone deserves the right to explain themselves before being put on "trial", so I'm going to try not to point fingers. My parents did many things that I would never do, but I can understand the trap they fell into with their addictions and empathize with how difficult it must have been for them.

My parents were young and foolish when I came into the picture. They did drugs, drank, and were involved with gangs, all of which are hard to escape. As a child, I couldn't tell my parents what to do. I didn't even know what was right or wrong!

They were supposed to be the responsible adults, yet they

didn't act like it. I always felt like I had to be the adult in the house.

I'm not trying to speak badly about my parents, but I think it is important to explain their situation so you understand where I'm coming from. Sometimes, when my mother wasn't home, my father would do drugs. He would try to mostly use when we weren't around, but even as a child, I noticed when his behavior wasn't normal. I noticed the crushed beer cans with holes and burn marks in them lying on the floor. I could infer what he was doing.

It wasn't all bad, though. I was the oldest child in the house at the time, and as a result, my mother let me do a lot of things that my younger siblings weren't allowed to do. I could drink soda with my dinner instead of waiting until I finished all my food. My sisters had to sit there and finish every bite before they got a sip. When it was time for my sisters to take a nap, my mom let me to stay awake.

Just because I had some perks, however, it didn't mean I wasn't terrified of my mother. I remember standing near her and shaking because I didn't know if she would start yelling or hit me for some random reason. You never knew when she would fly off the handle, and I was constantly on the lookout, ready for an attack.

When we went to visit family members, I wished for them to ask me to spend the night and hope my mom was in a good mood so she'd say yes. I was desperate for anything that would protect me from her for a little while. Falling asleep without fear or tears for one night was like heaven to me. I could let loose, and I didn't have to walk on eggshells. It a huge weight was taken off my chest, and I could breathe.

I used to be embarrassed of my mother. Wherever we went, she was loud, she said what was on her mind, and she didn't care what anyone else had to say. Ordinary outings, like going to the grocery store, would turn into a bad scene when my mom would get into altercations with strangers Most of the time, she was overreacting. A part of me wonders what she was feeling during these situations. What was causing her to feel so combative and on edge all the time? What was running through her mind?

My mom didn't talk about her childhood much—even to this day, there is a lot I don't know about my mom. I do know that her parents were from Texas and that they struggled with alcoholism—a habit my grandfather kicked—and that gang activity and violence were extremely prevalent throughout the family. My mother was the youngest daughter out of fourteen children. My mother and her siblings lost brothers, sons, cousins, and nephews to gang violence—surely these factors played into my mother's and her siblings' mental health and poor choices in life. Needless to say, these choices that I am referring to don't make them bad people. My family is very loving, but their past traumas have caused them to struggle.

One year, we had a joint birthday party for my sister Tiffany, my cousin, and me. My family wanted to sing "Happy Birthday" to all three of us at the same time. My mom wanted to sing to each of us individually. Something so simple should have been easily resolved with proper communication. However, that didn't happen.

Everyone decided to sing together, and my mom wasn't having it. She made a scene and told my sisters and I to gather our belongings and leave the family party without singing "Happy Birthday" or eating any cake. I was so embarrassed and upset. I felt a painful ache in my throat, but I knew if I cried or disagreed with my mom, it would lead to abuse that I didn't want to endure. My siblings and I knew the drill: we packed up, our heads hanging in shame and sadness, and followed my mom out of there. Things like this happened quite often. Nothing was ever normal or easy. Birthdays should be celebratory, filled with love and laughter. It wasn't like that for us, but what could we do about it? No one wanted to deal with my mother's antics.

My father never abused me like my mother did, but when he was mad, he would threaten to hit us. I learned to tune him out. He would always make rude comments or speak in a constant stream of slurred, drunken speech. I couldn't communicate or connect with him, which left me feeling abandoned and uncomfortable in his presence.

Whenever he spoke, I felt physically ill. I was so accustomed to drowning him out that even during the times where he might have been sober, I'd try not to listen to him.

I don't remember feeling hatred towards my father growing up, but I was embarrassed of him the same way I was with my mother. I remember hearing bad things about him from people around me, and I knew that they were true. People would call him an alcoholic, a junkie, a bad father, and a loser. They would judge him for his lack of a job, living situations, and his bad choices. I felt a deep sense of shame when I heard these things or whenever I had to go anywhere with him.

Despite this, I learned a lot from my father. He was a talented man. He was a phenomenal cook, a natural handyman, and he had a great personality when he was sober. He was funny, and most importantly, he had the biggest heart, which troubles me—he had the biggest heart, but he made some bad decisions, especially when it came to us. Can you be a good person but make bad choices? He had a big heart, but that didn't stop him from ending his addictions. He had a big heart, but couldn't get us the help we needed as a family.

My father was deep into his addictions when we were younger, and although he pulled away from his drug addiction, he was never able to kick his alcohol addiction. I could only imagine the life we would've had if he took control of the situation we were in much sooner. I didn't hate my father, but it was hard for me to love him—it still is.

I wish I would've tried to get to know my father when he was around. I'd love to know why he made the decisions he did. What held him back from being free from his struggles and addictions? Although it's too late to ask him directly, I am slowing finding out more and more about him and his childhood, his family in Alabama, the roots of his alcoholism, drug addiction, and poor mental health. While knowing more about him doesn't excuse his behaviors, it reminds me that he needed a lot of help and support that he just didn't receive—an issue that is quite common.

## What If My Parents Had Listened?

I always wonder how different things would've been if my parents hadn't lived the way they did. My mother's side of the family wasn't very discreet, and I overheard them tell my parents to get their act together many times. I heard them say things like, "Get yourself right," and "You're not okay, and your kids aren't okay," which confirmed to me that we weren't okay and that everyone definitely knew it.

I remember hearing my mother's parents, siblings, and other family members telling her to go to rehab or seek counseling, if not for her own sake, then for her children's, and reminding her that she was "better than this." My dad's side of the family would do the same, even threatening to call the DCFS if he didn't stop the drugs and abuse.

If I had a nickel for every time I heard the abbreviation DCFS growing up, I'd be pretty rich right about now. But it was all talk anytime that name came around; no one ever actually called, despite the many threats. I remember a family member actually giving me a card with the number on it at some point. She told me that I shouldn't hesitate to call if I ever needed to. I was afraid someone else would see it, so I kept the card hidden.

A part of me is upset that no one actually ever stepped in and called. They all knew what was going on.— Were they scared of my mother finding out who had reported her? Did they not really care? Were my sisters and I not worth saving?

Another part of me is grateful that they didn't call. God only knows where I would be right now if they did. Would my sisters and I have been taken from our parents and sent to live with a family member? Would they have taken us to a foster home? Would we have been separated even further from each other?

Sometimes I wonder what life would've been like if my parents had listened to others' advice. Would they have straightened up and got their stuff together? Would we have moved out of Pilsen? Would we have lived the life I dreamed of? Would my parents be together and happy? Would my father still be alive? Some questions I will never have answers for, and I just have to accept that I may never know. Nevertheless, I need to keep moving forward.

# CHAPTER 2:
# AFTER THE DIVORCE

**A**fter the divorce, my sisters and I bounced between my father and my mother. My sisters primarily lived with my mother and I lived with my father. While I was living with my father at Ray and Rochelle's place, my mother would constantly threaten to take me away. Often she would win the fight, and I would have to go with her against my will. No matter how much I screamed and cried, no matter how much Ray and Rochelle tried to negotiate with her and do what they could to get my dad on track, no matter how many times the police were called, legally, I had to go with my mom. She knew it and used it to her advantage. If my dad upset her, or if Ray and Rochelle didn't do what she wanted, she retaliated by removing me.

Adjusting to new and unfamiliar surroundings was hard for me. I would get used to living a certain way in a new environment, settling in and starting to feel safe and peaceful. Then I'd be removed from that place, often times in a traumatic way, and left to deal with the emotional toll. Yes, I loved my mother and my sisters, but I also loved my dad, Ray, and Rochelle. When I couldn't talk to them, I missed them, but that wasn't something I could tell my mom.

Living with my mother wasn't easy. She was now a single mom and worked many hours as a waitress at a truck stop. Since my mother worked so much to support us, we spent a lot of time with babysitters—one of my mother's sisters, most of the time. Nine times out of ten, they did not seem happy to watch us. This was probably because they already had so many of their own kids to watch, and adding three more kids to the mix was overwhelming. Since there were many kids to watch, and that meant there were a lot of kids to feed. Sometimes the meals would be tiny and wouldn't fill us up. Sometimes, there would be no meals at all.

One night I snuck into the kitchen and searched the fridge for anything I could get my hands on. The first thing I saw was a pack of tortillas. I grabbed a few and I stuffed my face quickly, trying not to get caught and not to choke on how cold, hard, and dry they were.

It seemed like we were struggling to survive—well, actually, we were. Struggling to survive meant that we would eat poor meals. It meant that we would wear the same clothes, even when they were dirty. It meant that when we got evicted from our house, we would sleep in our car. We would camp out in the parking lot that belonged to the bank a few lots next to the apartment building that we couldn't go back to. We were always startled when the security officer would come and tap his flashlight on the window, telling us we couldn't park there in the middle of the night.

"We have nowhere else to go," my mother would plead. But the end result was always my mom starting the car and pulling off to find a new place to park.

Once, my mother was in an argument with her boyfriend, and he started kicking the windshield of our car with his feet. My mother pleaded with him, "Please stop, you're going to break the window. My children sleep in this car, this is their home." It wasn't until that point that I realized that we really had nowhere else to go. We had nothing except our car, pillows, blankets, and each other.

On the days that we didn't have food, I remember my mother going to Jewel-Osco and buying a box of croissants and a six-pack of mini chocolate milk bottles. Now, that may be appealing to some as a snack, but when you haven't eaten all day, it is a lousy meal. It's days like those that made me feel like there was no hope in my life.

Someone once asked me, "After all your mom put you through, how are you still able to talk to her? I would still hold a grudge against her." My response was simple—how could I blame her for being a human being? I can't say this enough: my mom was doing all she could, and I feel like these were the times my siblings and I really learned to be grateful for what we did have—each other.

# CHAPTER 3:
# ROCHELLE AND RAY

After my mom lost our apartment in Pilsen, my dad won full custody of my sisters and me. My sisters moved in with my dad, his girlfriend Rachel, and her kids. I moved in with Ray and Rochelle. This was the part of my childhood when I saw my dad and my sisters the most. Rachel took good care of my sisters, and she was close with Rochelle, so we spent a lot of time at each other's houses. My sisters and I grew close to Rachel and her kids. To this day, my sisters and I consider them our siblings, and we look at Rachel as one of our moms. I knew my sisters were safe with them, and despite my dad's alcoholism, if he hadn't stepped up and gained custody of us, I don't know where we'd be.

It was around this time that my mother started her healing process and slowly stopped abusing my sisters and I. This was a major turning point in our relationship. When I spent holidays and weekends with my mom, she would treat me like a king. She let me eat anything and do whatever I wanted. I could tell that my mom loved having me with her. She would brag about my little accomplishments and introduce me to anyone she could. It made me feel good that she was proud of me—I felt seen by her, and I felt loved. It's all I had ever wanted, and she was able to give it to me ten times over. It's in those moments that I saw the mother she could have been if she had been able to keep it together for us. I think she saw that, too. It made me love her in a way I hadn't thought was possible before.

At this point, my mom was in a rebuilding stage in her life. Every time I visited her, she was in a new apartment and had a different job. At one point, she was living out of a motel. She was always barely making it and doing what she could to get by. It didn't matter to me. I never judged her. In fact, I was proud of her. I saw her trying to rebuild and change. Everything about her was different, even the way she talked and looked at me. I could see the sadness and regret when I looked into her eyes. Witnessing her change so dramatically inspired me and filled me with hope.

When she started to rebuild her life, whenever I wasn't with my mom, I missed her, but I enjoyed the moments I did have with her, and I look back on my time with her in those days with fondness. It was the beginning of a stronger, healthier relationship between us—one I had longed for since I was young. My mother, who had been through so much, was still fighting to get things right,—something I will always remember and be grateful for and would later fuel me when I made drastic changes in my life to be better for my own children. I love you, Mom.

My grandfather, as well as many other people, saw what my mom was going through. They wanted to help my mother get off of drugs and they wanted nothing but the best for us. My grandfather took us from my mother and wanted us to go and live with our father. So while my sisters went to live with my father, I went to live with my father's cousins, Rochelle and Ray. My father, who wasn't close to his brother, Steve, grew up with his cousins, and as the years grew they became his brothers and sisters, especially Ray and Rochelle.

Ray and Rochelle were not only special to my father, but they became special to me as well. It was them that first saw the way my parents were unstable. Well, it wasn't just them, but they were the only ones to act on it. They eventually convinced my parents to allow them to take care of me. My mother and father knew what the right thing to do was, and they probably made the smartest decision when they allowed my aunt and uncle to raise me.

Ray and Rochelle are brother and sister, but they became like a mother and father to me. I give them the credit for with raising me. Rochelle influenced the development of many of my positive qualities. Ray also taught me many things I needed to know about life, but he was much tougher on me.

When I lived with Ray and Rochelle, I felt much safer. Even though Ray yelled, neither of them ever hit me. I never felt like I was in the same kind of danger I was in when I lived with my parents.

I always viewed Ray as my main father figure, even while my actual father was still living. He taught me to be responsible and work hard. He would wake up early every day to go work and barely called off. He worked endless overtime to provide for us all and never thought twice about it or complained—he did it selflessly. He taught me that no matter how tired we were, we had to handle our responsibilities, such as tending to our home, cleaning, organizing, and any other obligations we had.

I picked up many of the hobbies and passions I have now from Ray. He loved music and cooking, which have become interests of mine, too. He taught me that trust and loyalty weren't always a given, but they could be earned. Above all, Ray showed me the value of putting your family first and loving them no matter what. Every night, no matter how tired he was, he cooked and ate dinner with us. Anytime we had some free time, we'd hop in the car and catch a show, go out to eat, or go shopping. Aside from that, we'd take family trips, go fishing, and attend a lot of family gatherings.

As much as I admire and respect Ray, I can see today that I picked up some of his bad habits, too. Ray has always had a temper and a short fuse. Whenever someone or something was bothering him, he let you know it. Like my mother, little things would make him explode.

Ray never put his hands on me, but I felt the same way around him that I felt around my mother—I was always walking on eggshells, constantly on edge, and never knew what would set him off.

Ray often spoke to others in a condescending, angry tone

of voice. I have vivid memories of him raising his voice at me or calling me names for not understanding or knowing how to do something. Patience wasn't his strong suit, to say the least. Many times, he took me asking for help as an invitation to yell at me. As a little boy, I felt scared, stupid, or worthless around him. This is something that affects me to this day—I catch myself speaking to my wife and children the same way he used to speak to me. As I look into the faces of my family, I see the same looks on their faces that I had when I was in their shoes. I can see their bodies tighten with tension. In them, I recognize that same sense of fear and unworthiness that I used to feel. It is something that I feel I can never overcome, and it makes me scared for the future of my family. I know they don't deserve it.

Does Ray's anger make him a bad person? Definitely not. I have learned to have empathy for him as I notice myself acting similarly. I don't mean to direct my anger at my family, but sometimes it just happens and it's the only way I know how to react.

Though Rochelle is my aunt, she has always been more like a mom to me. We have so much in common, like our great taste in music and our passion for reading, cooking, and writing. She has always been a rational person, and she knows the right thing to say in any situation. Rochelle is loving, safe, and wise—she is and will always be my heaven-sent angel.

Like Ray, Rochelle taught me many important life lessons that I now try to pass on to my own kids. She taught me the importance of saying what you feel, even when you're scared. She taught me to dive into my passions headfirst and to not let self-doubt hold me back. She encouraged me to explore every opportunity that came my way. Anytime I discussed a new hobby or idea of mine, she would help me figure out what I needed to do to achieve my goal. She never dismissed my thoughts and dreams, a kind of support every child should have.

Rochelle helped me to step out and have the courage and strength to shine, even in the darkness I was facing. She taught me about the things that truly matter: faith, love, honesty, integrity, perseverance, and self-confidence.

Was Rochelle a perfect parent growing up? No, and I don't expect any parents to be perfect. Like all of us, Rochelle made some mistakes and has said some things that I'm sure she wishes she could take back. Like Ray, she didn't have a lot of patience. She led a busy and scheduled life, and any inconveniences or delay would send her into a panic. And although her anger wasn't like Ray's, she let it get the best of her at times. But her intentions were always good—no doubt about that.

It wasn't until I started to settle in at Rochelle and Ray's that I broke out of my shell. By the time I graduated in eighth grade, I had made strides socially and had a group of friends. At that point, I had lived in the same neighborhood, Hegewisch, for five years, which helped.

Even though my relationships with my parents and my classmates began to improve, the fear that had been instilled in me in my formative years took some time to fade. The fear of my mother storming in to take me back, the fear of being abused, and the fear of not knowing where I would sleep that night slowly faded to only memories, but they would still pop back up once in a while. I would have vivid nightmares almost every night, and would wake up dripping with sweat, shaking, screaming, and soaked in a pool of my own urine until I was fifteen. I tried going to doctors and taking different medications, but nothing helped. I just had to wait it out, and I eventually grew out of it. I don't know how or why I did—I must have finally felt safe.

# Part II
*Early Adulthood*

# CHAPTER 4:
# THE CHOICE

**M**y whole life, I've always felt like I've had to defend my mother. With all the bad decisions she's made throughout her life, she's left a bad taste in many people's mouths. As her son, I witnessed everything about my mother firsthand—her struggles, highs, lows, failed relationships, and everything in between. However, never did I ever call her any of the names I heard others calling her: a bad mom, a bitch, fat, ugly, a crackhead, a loudmouth, a drug addict, a loser, unlovable, unworthy, a burnout—just to name a few. My mother was always the subject of mockery.

As a child and a teen, hearing these vile words never sat well with me. Even though those words were directed at my mom, they hurt as if I was the one being called those names. When I could, I would try and defend her, but I didn't always feel like I could. I got angry. How could people speak so harshly toward her? Especially with her son standing there? I felt worthless. Those vicious words weren't directed towards me, but I was a reflection of my mother, and I knew that even at a young age. Even as I'm writing this, I can feel that pit in the bottom of my stomach. Nausea, dazed and confused, like needles under my skin, cold, and shaky—these were common feelings for me as a young child, and unfortunately I feel these feelings to this day any time I'm in an uncomfortable situation.

I had a choice to make: would I join others and believe their harsh words? Or would I continue to love my mother, no matter what the truth was? Would I disown her as my mother? Would I choose to never forgive her?

Luckily, I was able to empathize with my mother, and I never let the hate that was projected towards her stick to me and change my thoughts toward her. I will always know what my mother is: a human who made mistakes, who had struggles that she didn't overcome, and didn't receive the help she needed. However, to this day, I feel like this choice is haunting me. I am still reminded of her many mistakes by those around me as if I still have this choice to disown her, but my mind is still made up. There are a lot of people who hold on this bad image of my mother in their minds. A lot of people who have yet to forgive her for her transgressions and hold onto that hate and negative feelings towards her. But that's okay, because I choose to love her. I choose to forgive her. I choose to help her move on from her past, despite what others may say. I choose to have her in my life and in my children's life. I choose love, hope, and forgiveness.

Besides the choice to improve my relationship with my mother, I had another choice to make as a child and as a young adult. The way I see it I have two mothers—my biological mother and Rochelle. As a child, I was in a constant battle to pick a side.

Growing up, I would listen to them bad-mouth each other. I would be caught in the middle their fights, and I felt so confused. As a child, I didn't see right or wrong—I just wanted to be able to love them both and to not have to worry about showing more love to one than the other.

I always had to make sure I spent time with both my mom and Rochelle on holidays. When there were any major events, I had to make sure they were both there. I couldn't even properly enjoy these holidays and major events because of the constant guilt I felt. Sadly, that feeling follows me to this day. When my kids were born, it only made my guilt and anxiety worse. Not only were they both my mothers, but now they were both my children's grandmothers.

This was so hard for me to think about. Would my children be dragged into this same mindset—that they had to choose between my mom and Rochelle? Luckily my children, like myself, are full of love. They have great relationships with both my mother figures and don't feel the need to pick sides. They know them as their grandmas, and the rest is irrelevant. One day, I hope I feel like there is no choice to be made—I can have both my mothers, and my children can have both their grandmothers. Love, hope, and forgiveness can be my choice, my children's choice, and my family's choice.

My mother and Rochelle's relationship took a turn for the better when my father passed in 2009. There is a saying that death brings people closer together, and in this case, it did. Life is too short to hold grudges and cling to the past. Death reminds us of this.

At the end of the day, both my mother and Rochelle have done so much for me, and they are my two biggest supporters. Today, they get along, encourage each other, and occasionally spend time together. The shift in their relationship didn't happen overnight, and it's not perfect. But it's a major improvement, and it certainly takes a huge weight off my shoulders.

In addition to Rochelle and my biological mother, I grew to see Rachel as a mother figure when she came into our lives. When Rachel came into the picture, she and Rochelle grew to be very close. To this day, they still refer to each other as sisters. That was great for them, but it was bad for my mom, because at times, it felt like two against one.

No matter what I did, I felt as if I couldn't win with any of them. When I graduated from high school, everyone was so proud of me. I was Senior Class President, I was heading to college, and I hadn't given anyone an ounce of trouble. Rochelle wanted to give me a graduation party, and I was excited, but also nervous, because I didn't know if my mom would be welcomed. I think Rochelle could sense my fear. She tried to consider my feelings and just wanted me to be happy.

In the end, my mom was invited, and I couldn't wait for my party. The big day finally came, and it was exactly how I knew it would be—my mom off to the side by herself while our other family and friends hung out with my sisters. When the family took turns giving speeches, everyone clapped, and the room was filled with love.

When my mom gave her speech, you could feel a shift in the room. Most of the family and friends in attendance didn't know too much about my mom, only the stories they had heard about her and our past. I don't think they didn't knew what to expect. It's hard to explain, but I understood why they felt the way they did, and after so many years of seeing Rochelle, Ray, and my father go through tough things with my mom, the family took their side. In our family, no one's quiet about how much they dislike someone. No one was giving my mom a chance to show how much she changed. It hurt my feelings, but I couldn't wait for my mom to leave. Not because I didn't want her there, but because her being there was uncomfortable. My mom wasn't good at reading the room, but on some level, I know she felt it this time. I could see it in her body language, I could hear it in her voice. She was surrounded by my family, but no one in the room was *her* family, except for my siblings and me. She was there to support me, and although she felt out of place, she still stayed to show support for her son and his accomplishment.

That being said, things as joyful as my daughter's birth and baptism were still overshadowed by the competition between my mom and Rochelle. When you're in the thick of it and you can't see outside of your own emotions, you're unable to think about how those emotions affect other people. My mother figures didn't understand how their rivalry affected me and I hated every moment of their interactions, because even when they were playing nice, the tension was so thick, I felt like I was suffocating.

# CHAPTER 5:
# HIGH SCHOOL AND COLLEGE

When I was a young teenager, I hadn't thought much about moving on from the past. I was focused on trying to find my place in the world and figure out what my future would look like. I started breaking out of my shell more, and I realized the value of working hard.

## Passing of My Father

My father passed away during my freshman year of high school. During the last few months of his life, he had been living with me at Ray and Rochelle's house. He had fallen down the stairs and broken his neck and was in a halo cast for his final months.

Fortunately, many things stayed the same when my father moved in with us. My father wasn't the head of the household, and I could still rely on Ray and Rochelle.

A part of me liked having my father in the house, but it wasn't exactly a walk in the park. His condition didn't inspire him to want to change his life or stop his bad habits. Instead, he leaned into them even more. He started taking more pills, and he continued his constant drinking.

At one point, Ray kicked my father out of the house for a week or two due to his behavior. No one knew where he went during that time. It was a scary time for me, and I was concerned for my father. He wasn't communicating with any of us. I remember being so upset when he was kicked out, but it wasn't my house or my rules. I felt helpless.

I did what I could to try to make sure my father was safe. I would call him every day to try to figure out where he was. Whenever I was riding in the car, I would look out the window, hoping to catch a glimpse of him. It was a sad time for me, but I was used to these feelings. My father had always lived dangerously and irresponsibly, and at the end of his life, he was no different.

I was quiet and observant, and I felt there was nothing I could do to help my father or stop him from continuing down this dark path. It wasn't that I didn't have anything to say or didn't know what to say. Believe me, I had a lot to say! Yet, I wondered what the point would be in saying something. I knew I would be wasting my breath.

When I learned that my father passed away, I didn't know what to think. Everything after it happened was a blur. The night before he passed, Ray and Rochelle had a huge party with friends and family from all over the city. The night was filled with laughter, food, alcohol, and a lot of love. My father was always the life of the party, and on that night, he took the stage and pulled out all his jokes and dance moves. A part of me wonders if he knew that was going to be his last night. He was barely recovering from his neck injury, but didn't seem to be in much pain that night as he laughed, sang, drank, ate, and shared his love. Above everything else that happened that night, the memory that will forever remain in my soul is the toast my father made.

"To my only son, TJ, I am so proud of you. I love you, son," he said as he kissed me on the head.

"I love you too, dad," I told him. Little did I know that would be the last time we would ever hear each other say those words. Up until that point, there was only a handful of times I had told my father that I loved him, and they were usually situations where I was forced to say, "Yeah, love you too." But that night was different, and the "I love you" I gave to my father was genuine and from my heart.

That night, we all went to bed fulfilled. I remember feeling the energy in the air that night before bed, everyone so happy and cheerful. As our family slowly started to wake, we mingled and recapped the party. Then my stepbrother, Jose, one of Rachel's sons from her previous relationship, came running up the stairs in a panic to inform us my father was unresponsive. I remember the adults all running down to the basement where my father was while I sat in shock. The world stopped moving—I could feel my stomach turning, sweat forming, and tears ready to explode out of me like never before.

My childhood had haunted me my whole life like an unwanted shadow. I was always able to keep going with my trauma buried beneath the surface, but then my father passed away. His passing was very painful and brought up many painful memories and regrets.

My father, unlike my mother, never grew out of his drinking phase. Times like his last night aside, I almost always hated being around him. He was always drunk, and that also meant he was unsafe and unpredictable.

The blessing was that my relationship with my father had improved towards the end of his life, in part because we spent more time together—but that meant it was all the more painful when I lost him.

Since my father had been absent from my life growing up and was now completely gone, I began to turn to my substitute fathers and mentors. One of those men was Larry, who I'd known for over a decade.

I was fifteen when I first met him. It was June or July of 2009, and my brother's girlfriend was the manager of a restaurant called Hienie's Chicken. She got me an interview with Larry, who was the owner.

I was nervous when I went in for my interview, but when I met Larry, we immediately connected. I did my best to make a good impression on him. It was important to me to get the job. My father had passed away just a month or two before, and I felt the need to step up and take on some responsibilities.

I was excited to learn I had got the job, and I decided to dedicate myself to it. I started off working in the back, making pizzas and sandwiches, bagging and taking orders, and answering the phone. I worked hard and eventually became a manager.

Larry had come from a very poor family and had taken many

risks. He understood my situation, and he had compassion for me. He also challenged me. Larry taught me how to be a better employee and person and how to work well, have fun, live my life, and be successful.

I worked at Hienie's Chicken until 2015, when I felt the need to move on. Even when I left, I still went back to help out because I had grown very close to Larry. He had become like a father to me. We're still close to this day. He treats me like a son, and we talk almost daily. If I have a bad day, I call him and share what's going on in my life. I ask him for advice and lean on him for support.

Larry is also the godfather to my daughter. I was working for him when she was born, and my wife and I asked him and his then-wife, Denise, to be her godparents. We knew there would be no better couple to help guide our daughter through life with great morals and beliefs.

Larry has seen me through my worst and my best times. He always reminds me that the best things in life can't be bought. Instead, the best things in life are the moments when we are surrounded by those we care about. Larry is the most humble, honest, caring, God-loving, and genuine men I have ever met, and I am extremely grateful to have him in my life.

## Academics

After my father passed away, I began to turn my academics around. During my sophomore year, I was on the verge of being kicked out of the International Baccalaureate, an advanced academic program. I worked hard and was able to raise my grades enough to stay in the program. This experience was a huge achievement for me, and it motivated me throughout the rest of high school. IB taught me self discipline, motivation, and organization. The program is intense and required a lot of its students to stay in good standings. Participation was crucial in the curriculum, and the workload was massive. We learned to think analytically and were challenged to think outside the box. Many colleges take a closer look at IB students who've applied. That was important to me because it motivated me to attend college.

From then on, I was extremely academically driven. I had learned how to apply myself and not give up, and it gave me hope when I saw the positive results. Even though I couldn't control other parts of my life, for once, it felt like my fate was in my own hands and I could reach my goals.

During my junior year of high school, I was accepted into a summer internship program at the Illinois State Treasurer's Office. This was a huge achievement for me because politics was my passion. I was able to work with the Invest in Illinois Division, where I conducted research and collaborated on and provided content for presentations related to the Linked Deposit and ICash programs. Since I was only seventeen, it gave me great early exposure to not only the political landscape, but also the corporate world, because the office I worked in functioned in many similar capacities.

When my internship ended, the office had a little ceremony for the interns. I was there alongside interns who were in college, and I was amongst the one or two still in high school. I felt this incredible sense of pride and accomplishment when I received a recognition award for being a part of the internship program. We took a picture with the state treasurer, and to this day, it hangs on the wall in Rochelle's dining room.

When I was a senior in high school, I was accepted into the National Honors Society. Being a member of a prestigious society meant a lot to me, so I worked and studied hard. There were sleepless nights and endless hours of homework, research, and studying. There were times I wanted to give up, but I knew if I just pushed myself a little harder, I could do it. I wanted so badly to have the privilege of including my membership on my college applications. When you have struggled through life with low self-esteem and feel unseen and unheard, there's both validation and tremendous joy in something like that.

That same year, I was elected student council president. I knew winning would look great on my college applications but it was also something I knew would give me a voice and exposure to how politics work within an educational setting. I had already begun to feel this pull towards politics, and it seemed like a good way to not only learn more about it, but also to hopefully have a hand in making strategic changes for the student body. I already had strong relationships with my teachers and counselors, so that gave me an advantage. The position involved public speaking, working with the school administration, engaging with the student body, fundraising, event planning, and learning to network with other organizations outside of the school. One of my proudest moments was working with the rest of the council on a citywide attendance initiative.

Being the student council president helped me step out of my comfort zone. I liked being the center of attention sometimes, but this was an entirely new level.

I was also one out of fifteen students in my class who were invited to attend the senior class trip to Spain. This was a great honor and an amazing experience. We were gone a total of ten days and visited five cities. We explored Spanish culture by enjoying the local cuisine, visiting castles and historic landmarks, taking in the beautiful scenery, and learning to flamenco dance. Being in Spain was one of the best experiences I have ever had, and it was the perfect way to end my high school experience. My dream is to return to Spain many times so my family can experience it, and eventually, I plan on retiring there.

## Sports

Playing sports in high school also helped me get out of my shell. It was difficult at first because I've always struggled with self confidence. Others sometimes saw me as cocky or arrogant, but the truth is that I was nervous and scared on the inside. I never fully recovered and nervousness and fear that followed me from my traumatic childhood. I had a great way of projecting a fake me who was always confident and "had it all together," but in reality, I was scared, nervous, and very self-conscious. So yes, to some I may have seemed arrogant and cocky, but they had no idea who the real me was.

Playing sports helped me to get out of my head and forced me to connect with my body and those around me. It opened many new doors for me, and I was able to make friends. I played football, ran track, wrestled, and competed on a bowling team.

I learned the importance of working hard and pushing myself to overcome my self-doubt. I was nervous about joining each sports team because I thought that all the other athletes were great and that I couldn't ever compete with them. They were in shape, fast, and they knew their games well, I was always the rookie. This meant I had to push myself harder than everyone else so that I could get in shape and improve my skills to become a valuable teammate. Despite my inexperience and intimidation, I soon learned playing sports isn't about competing with your teammates, but playing alongside them. We all had different backgrounds and hobbies, but none of that mattered when we were at practice or a game. I learned the importance of teamwork and how to fit in with a new crowd, lessons which I have carried with me into my career.

At the end of my high school career, I was accepted to the college I wanted to attend, North Park University, a Christian liberal arts university in Chicago. I chose North Park initially because a good friend of mine decided he wanted to go there to play football, so I started looking into it, and something about it just felt right to me. He didn't end up going there, but I still pursued it. When I opened my acceptance letter with trembling hands, I could hardly believe it—all of my hard academic work had paid off. It was a proud day when I received that letter and gladly accepted. It was like something inside me was missing, and when I attended the open house for the first time, something just felt so fulfilling to me. I knew that this is where I was meant to be. I had to drop out of college during my junior year to provide for my family, but the time I spent at school was an amazing experience and achievement, especially since I was the first member of my immediate family to go to college.

At North Park, I became the chapter president for an organization called the Young Leaders Alliance. We held events and took on projects that pushed for change and less violence in Chicago, and educated members of low income communities on the resources available to them. One of our recurring projects was organizing neighborhood take-backs, where the members of our group rallied to improve communities where there was violence and health risks that were being ignored by the city of Chicago. Our chapter was able to meet with the mayor and other persons in positions of power to share our concerns about some of the changes that needed to be made.

I loved going into communities that were notorious among outsiders for their high crime rates and discovering the people that really lived there. I met people who were just as concerned about the violence and other problems in their neighborhoods as we were, and I saw communities come together in meaningful ways.

YLA's motto was "Power to the Village," inspired by the saying, "it takes a village to raise a child." While I was part of the organization, I discovered the power of the "village," and I have carried that lesson with me to this day. I've seen how people can make a difference when they come together, and it inspires me to help people to do that.

I've learned that it takes a village to stand up and change a community. When we try to tackle the major problems that people are facing all over the world all on our own, we fail. Without support, no one has enough resources and power to address things like gun violence, corrupt politics, drug abuse, alcohol abuse, starvation, and limited access to essentials like food and water. When people stand up together, they can take charge of their fate. As a village-like organization, YLA had the power to change neighborhoods, and we did.

Since dropping out of college, I'm proud to say that I've been able to work hard and earn enough to support my family. I've been successful in every job I've had, earning promotions and management positions in almost all of them. I've been able to achieve success, even without a full college degree. Many have told me that I couldn't accomplish my dreams without that piece of paper, and at times, I have felt like they were right. But deep down, I know the plan God has put in my heart doesn't require a degree, and that my family will still love me without it.

# CHAPTER 6:
# LEARNING TO FORGIVE

In my twenty-nine years on this earth, I've learned how to forgive. It's been a long journey, but a necessary step in the healing process for me. I believe everyone deserves a second chance and the right to be forgiven. The two people I've had to work the hardest to forgive are my parents. While I don't deny that their mistakes had a big impact on my life, those mistakes no longer control me and will not determine my path.

## Finding Faith and Hope

Faith has been an important part of my life since I was young. I was raised in the Catholic church, though we hardly ever attended services. When things got bad at home, I prayed. I believed that God would hear me and that He could make a difference. I never knew exactly what to say, but I hung on to faith. When you're beaten and broken, sometimes that's all you have. He is the God of the broken.

The first time I felt close to God was at a church called Pilsen Assembly of God. My mother and siblings would visit the church weekly, and when I would have visitations with her over the weekend, she would take us on Sundays. I didn't really understand what Pastor Andrew was saying—maybe I wasn't really paying attention to the word of God and was focusing on my mom instead. But it was at this point that I witnessed the love, hope, and forgiveness that God gave. I didn't quite understand it, but I knew what I was feeling was right.

I saw my mom believe in something more those days. She showed me that despite our *many* failures, mistakes, and bad choices, despite our finances or living situations, we were loved. That's when I knew that my mom was trying, and that's when I knew she was struggling. Struggling from living a life she didn't want, struggling from beating herself up for her mistakes and flaws. In return, God gave her what she needed. God gave her what every parent should give their children: love, hope, and forgiveness. Unconditionally.

It was the first time I really felt a connection to the church and to God. When we walked into the church, we were greeted politely by many people. Everyone seemed so genuine and caring—it's like they knew to tread lightly with us. During the service, I watched people sing, cry, pray, and hug. That's when I realized that there were so many people out there that were hurting. I realized that there were safe spaces that people could go to without judgement. We weren't the only the messed up people in the world, and our struggle was a lot more common than I thought.

It wasn't until college that my relationship with God blossomed into a more serious commitment. There, my mind was opened to an environment where thousands of students my age all believed in something bigger than themselves and all had a different connection to God. People from all walks of life and who all had different life experiences who were showered in the love of God. I learned about God's love and forgiveness as if it was the first time. I started reading my Bible and growing in my faith, always longing to know more. Believing that just like those around me, I was worthy of His love. My family was worthy also.

Faith helped me realize that it was okay to be vulnerable. I had got used to immediately distrusting others in order to protect myself, but my faith helped me open up to others and connect. My faith and the friendships I formed because of Christianity helped me realize that no matter how beaten and broken I was, I was worth loving. Realizing that I could be loved in spite of anything I may have done was an amazing feeling. So was the idea that I could learn to love those who had hurt me.

It was empowering to know that God loved me and that He was in my corner. God's love opened my mind to endless possibilities. I realized my life could be so much better than I ever thought and there was hope. I wasn't a beaten and broken little boy anymore. I wasn't starving and helpless anymore. I was a son of God, and with him on my side, I knew that everything was going to be okay.

## Forgiving My Mother

Realizing I needed to learn to forgive my mother wasn't easy. She had abused my siblings and I in unspeakable ways, but I loved her, and I wanted to have a real relationship with her. In order to do that, I had to forgive her. The hate that I once felt and fear I once had for her didn't have a place in me anymore—it all turned to love.

After my mother had started to clean up her act, I saw people treating her badly. Our family couldn't leave behind the image they had of the person she once was in order to see the changes in the person she had become—but I could. Everyone seemed to want me to hate her and treat her like she wasn't even a person, but I didn't think that was right. I rebelled by learning to forgive her. I had realized my mother wasn't a monster—she was a human being, in need of love as much as I, my sisters, or anyone else does.

Despite the many, many mistakes she made over the years, I saw that she was beginning to change and trying to be a better person. I wanted to encourage and be there for my mother as she made these important steps.

## Forgiving My Father

I will always regret that I didn't forgive my father while he was still alive. I didn't even think about it until it was too late. We were never really on bad terms with each other, but that was mostly because we didn't have much of a relationship. The truth is, you can't have a substantive, healthy relationship with someone who's drinking all the time. Under the surface, however, resentment was always boiling inside me. I doubt that my father ever realized that because I tried to act kind and be peaceful when I saw him.

Did I resent my father for all the ways he impacted my life and childhood negatively? Yes, but I also loved him. It's amazing to realize that you can love someone even though you can't stand being around them ninety-nine percent of the time.

## Forgiving Myself

One of the most important healing steps I have taken has been to learn how to forgive myself. I've learned the hard way that there are some people in life who won't forgive you. You can't make everyone happy—someone is always going to be mad at you for something, whether or not the problem or hurt you caused was intentional.

I don't want to go through life begging for forgiveness from other people. I never asked for forgiveness from my mother or father because I didn't need it. I hadn't wronged my parents, but they had wronged me. So why did I feel so guilty? Why did I feel like I needed to be forgiven?

Even though I was the victim, I had to forgive myself like I was the perpetrator. I could have easily carried a grudge against my parents for my whole life, hating everyone and everything just because of how hard my childhood was. But where is the joy in that? What benefit do we gain from holding in grudges against people who have hurt us?

Instead, I learned to live intentionally, telling myself that even though things had been hard, and even though people had done harm to me, I could still move forward with my own life. I had the power to make my own path, and I had the power to forgive myself for allowing my struggles to stop me or slow me down.

Self-forgiveness isn't just saying sorry to yourself. It's wholeheartedly allowing yourself to be free from any harm that has been done to you. Self-forgiveness is when you are able to tell yourself that even though people haven't apologized to you, you can still forgive them.

You can't heal if your wound is still open, so do yourself a favor and forgive yourself. Have the courage to move forward, accepting that you will make mistakes. Have the courage to move forward, knowing that people will hurt you in the future, too. Have the courage to forgive yourself, even when other people can't forgive you.

It's easy to get wrapped up in the past and how horrible it was. It's easy to go through life trapped in self-punishment. Let it go, my friend!

# PART III
*My Life Today*

# CHAPTER 7:
## MY NEW MOTIVATIONS

Throughout my life, I have had many passions and hobbies. Through my hobbies, I have identified my strengths and weaknesses, and I've developed as a person. I have realized the value of diving deep into something and growing my skills over time.

My hobbies and outlets have also given me the courage to step out of my comfort zone. I have learned that no matter what situation I am in, I can try my hardest and do the best I can with what I have. It taught me that I didn't have to be perfect—I just had to follow my desires and stick to them. With practice, determination, and patience, I could master anything I put my mind to. I didn't have to be perfect. I just had to be satisfied with my own abilities and progress.

Cooking has been a great outlet for me. When I'm in the kitchen, it's like nothing else matters. I love to lose myself in the creative process. I scrounge around my kitchen and work with what I have to create something tasty. I love making people happy with my meals. There's something about cooking that puts me at ease. Maybe it's the way that it takes my mind off of things for a little while. One of my biggest passions is to serve, whether I'm in the kitchen or interacting with customers. I love meeting people from all over the world and listening to their stories. It's fun for me to please groups of people, and I love being the reason people have a good time.

My father loved to cook, and although I never really wanted to be around him, I did enjoy the meals he provided. In the final years of his life, he cooked less and less. Unfortunately, his meals are just a vague memory to me now. I am constantly reminded by family of his cooking abilities, and it helps me remember what his food tasted like and to unbury the memories I had hidden in my mind.

## Where I Am Today

As I get older, I become more aware of my feelings. I used to feel unworthy, like I wasn't good enough and would never amount to anything. I thought I didn't deserve to be loved because of everything I went through.

As an adult, this started affecting my own family. I allowed those feelings to control me. I had never learned how to deal with these emotions, and I thought my wife and children were the cause of them. I found myself screaming and yelling at them and not being there for them emotionally. I repeated patterns from the family I grew up in.

As a child, my family would say things like, "you'll never amount to anything," "you're not using your brain," "you're stupid," or "you're not trying hard enough."

"You are worthy, you are smart, you are loved": those were the things I needed to hear.

Now, I'm trying to create that kind of positive atmosphere in my family. I want my children to believe in themselves, and that they can do anything they put their minds to. I want my children to know they are loved, they are worthy, and that I care about them.

Now, I try hard to be a better husband and father. I try to be a better person every day. It's hard to change the unhealthy patterns I was following, especially when I'm dealing with my own struggles of anxiety and depression. But I want to build my family up, not tear them down. I want to guide them and support them. I want to help them to build positive mental habits.

Even though we all face personal battles, these battles don't make us lesser people. We're all unique, and no one is exactly like you. We all have something special to offer to the world and others that no one else has, and we have to realize that.

## My Goals for a Better Future

I'm always trying to create better mental, physical, and spiritual habits. For a while, I felt stuck and didn't know where to start. When I started going to therapy, it was the catalyst for me to get my life back on track. Today, I have many goals I am working towards one day at a time.

## Mental Health Goals

Right now, my life revolves around mental health struggles, since I battle anxiety every day. In the future, I want to feel free, like I'm not trapped inside my mind all of the time. I want to feel safe inside my mind, with less judgmental thoughts and more positivity.

Even though I see my progress every day, and I remind myself that my anxiety and depression won't just disappear. It takes a lot of effort to get mentally stable, it's not something that you can just switch on and off. I have to choose to live intentionally every day because without purpose it's hard to fall off track. It's choosing to rewire all the old habits that I've lived with since a child and reframe them to a new way of thinking. I may not be perfect and I never will be, but, I know that by living intentionally I will get closer to where I need to be.

## Spiritual Health Goals

I've been working on my relationship with God. I've tried to change how I talk to Him and what I talk to Him about in my day-to-day life. I try to be honest and realistic with God, which forces me to be honest with myself as well.

It helps to know I am unconditionally loved by God and that I have a purpose. As I talk to God, I feel His acceptance and know I can be myself.

I was listening to a sermon by Joel Osteen the other day. He was talking about people who keep focusing on trying to heal themselves, and he was saying it's better to focus on healing others. That really spoke to me because I've always been passionate about helping others.

As a kid, I wanted to be a therapist and study psychology.

At different stages of my life, I wanted to serve in the army, be a pastor, or be a police officer. The common theme among those jobs is service. Even when I dabbled in politics, I was focused on service and helping others.

As I've become aware of my desire to help others, I thought maybe if I focus on that, and I will heal along the way. I'm not saying we should overextend ourselves to help others—I still need boundaries, but I can push myself to be a positive influence on someone's life.

I can help others in little ways, such as giving positive encouragement. Sometimes just doing little things can help people feel better about themselves.

## Taking Practical Steps to Help Others

One practical step I took in this direction was to start a support group to create an open dialogue around mental health and to allow safe spaces for both men and women to come and share their journeys and learn from others and support one another. In these groups we discuss not only our journeys but also we learn coping skills, stress skills, healthy habits, boundaries, positive feelings and so much more. This has been especially important for the men. Men don't talk about their problems because there's this idea that we need to be big, strong men. We're told to "man up" and "be a man," but what does that mean? Emotions are associated with weakness, and men are therefore discouraged from sharing them. Are men supposed to hold in all their emotions and just keep pushing forward? Should they hold in all the things that trigger and bother them?

In the culture I grew up in, adults talked down to their children, husbands talked down to their wives, and the topic of mental health was off-limits. As I've become more emotionally healthy, I've realized that this is not okay. I don't want other men to continue the harmful patterns they grew up in. I want to build them up and show them it's okay to be vulnerable.

Bottling up your feelings only makes things worse. You need to talk about them!

I'm all for the either the man or the woman being the head of the household, but no matter what roles the man plays, a father should be building up his family and encouraging them. Men should be mental and spiritual leaders teaching good morals and values to their children. Men need to set a good example by being self-aware and accepting. How can we emotionally support our families if we can't even build ourselves up?

Another practical step I'm taking is hosting a series of events focused on the topic of men's mental health. I want to raise awareness and normalize men talking about these kinds of issues. I want people to know that it doesn't make us less-than if we have mental health struggles. It's nothing to be ashamed of.

I want people to challenge themselves to turn their negative thoughts around. If we keep focusing on these negative thoughts, our lives will turn gray. We all need a little more sunshine in our lives.

They say it takes a village to raise a child, but it also takes a village to raise someone up when they're down. We need to support our own communities and have more compassion, hope, and patience with ourselves and each other. We need to be mindful of what we say and who we are saying it to. You never know what others are facing. We all have the power to make someone else's day better or worse, and we all need to choose which we want to do.

## Words of Wisdom from Tommy Talks

Tommy Talks originally started as a blog to help me share my thoughts about mental health and to share my personal journey with it. After I started getting out into the community, I realized that a lot of people were in need of more help and information, so I turned my blog into a 501c3 nonprofit organization. Our goal is to normalize and promote improved mental health by providing education, peer support, and creative arts outlets for all.

The Tommy Talks community is built on collaboration between community leaders and organizations, business owners, and friendships. To date, Tommy Talks has hosted over two dozen events, such as our pop-up series "You Are Not Alone," "Light the Night," "Let's Go Fishing," just to name a few. At these events, the goal is to invite everyone in and showcase different forms of healing and coping. Positive coping does not look the same for everyone, so we try to lead our guests to a variety resources, including playing games and doing activities that promote positive coping, including mindfulness, yoga, meditation, talking, and learning. We share our experiences, our struggles, our successes, because when it's all said and done, I wholeheartedly believe we're better when we live authentically and intentionally. We can learn from each other and be better because of it. These pop-ups are just a start for the community work we have in store, including a mentorship program that focuses on teaching positive coping skills and improving mental health; a CPS program for parents and children to take together that teaches positive communication in families and how to break generational curses; a program for children of alcoholic parents; and so much more.

Doing this work has taught me many lessons. It's helped me see how important thought patterns are. If we are feeding our minds with thoughts like, "I'm not good enough," or if we have a victim mentality of "why do I have bad luck?" "why can't I move forward?" or "why do I keep getting the short end of the stick?" then it will become a self-fulfilling prophecy.

Sometimes we believe we are worthless, that we will always be by ourselves, or that we will never get a wife and kids. The truth is, we tell our bodies and minds what to do. If you tell yourself to jump, you'll jump. If you tell yourself you'll never be of value, your body won't let you be of value. You start to believe the things you keep thinking. You tell yourself you'll never be happy like someone else, yet you don't know what that person is going through. We are all valuable, and if we don't start picking ourselves up, no one will. If we keep waiting for the right time to do better, it won't happen. If you don't work for something, you won't get it. You need to tell yourself you can do something and remember that you're not your mom, and you're not your dad. You're not trapped by the patterns of alcohol or abuse in your family. You have the power to break free from all of that, and it starts by taking things one step at a time, starting today.

Everyone's always worried about being perfect or being the best. I challenge you not to strive for perfection, but for progress. Enjoy the little steps that will help you get to where you want to be. You'll never be perfect, but you'll always live in progress. Think about what you are thankful for, what you're good at, and what makes you happy. Find those things and do them.

# CHAPTER 8:
# LEARNING ABOUT AND HEALING FROM ABUSE

Though I would like to believe that my story is not the norm, the truth is that child abuse is a widespread problem. Each year, almost 700,000 children are abused in the United States alone, and over a thousand of them will die. 2.7% of children one year old and under are abused every year. As many as 78% of children who suffer neglect and abuse do so at the hands of their parents.[1] These are sobering numbers, and they mean that we as a society need to be more aware of abuse and take steps to prevent it.

## Monitoring for Behavioral Signs of Abuse

There are many behavioral issues a child can develop as a result of being abused. Adults need to do their part by being aware of these signs and investigating further when they see them. Here are some signs that a child might be a victim of abuse:

- *Excessive crying as an infant*
- *Developmental delays*
- *Clinginess or acting overly fearful and anxious*
- *Development of phobias*
- *Recurring nightmares or sleeping problems*
- *Wetting the bed, especially as an older child*
- *Social withdrawal*
- *Hyperactivity*
- *Poor concentration*
- *Noticeable decrease in academic performance*
- *Frequent absences from school*
- *Speech disorders*

---

1. https://www.nationalchildrensalliance.org/media-room/national-statistics-on-child-abuse/

- *Regressive behaviors (Ex. thumb-sucking, talking like a baby)*
- *Fear of a parent*
- *Disordered eating*
- *Appearing depressed and passive*
- *Verbally abusive or physically aggressive behavior towards others*
- *Damaging objects or harming pets*
- *Substance abuse*
- *Self-harm*
- *Shying away from touch*
- *Flinching at sudden noises or movements*
- *Over-compliance* [2]
- *Acting on guard at all times*
- *Fear of going home*
- *Wearing long sleeves, pants, or scarves (perhaps to cover up injuries)* [3]

## Physical and Medical Signs of Abuse

Sometimes children can develop health problems due to the stress of abuse on their bodies. Here are some physical ailments that might indicate abuse, especially if they are recurring and there are no other obvious causes:

- *Headaches*
- *Chronic or acute abdominal pain*
- *Expressing that something chronically hurts*
- *Asthma, or worsening preexisting asthma*
- *Regular sore throat*
- *Noticeable weight gain or loss*
- *Difficulty or pain with movement*
- *Vomiting and irritability*[4]

2. "Signs and Symptoms of Abuse/ Neglect." Stanford Medicine. Accessed April 1, 2021. https://childabuse.stanford.edu/screening/signs.html
3. https://www.helpguide.org/articles/abuse/child-abuse-and-neglect.htm
4. "Signs and Symptoms of Abuse/ Neglect." Stanford Medicine. Accessed April 1, 2021. https://childabuse.stanford.edu/screening/signs.html

- *Signs of malnutrition*
- *Weight loss*
- *Poor hygiene*
- *Malnutrition*
- *Fractures, dislocations, or bruising*
- *Bites (especially human ones)*
- *Unexplained burns*
- *Unexplained cuts*
- *Excessive hair loss*
- *Facial or head injuries*
- *Hemorrhaging*
- *A subdural hematoma*
- *Trauma to abdominal organs*[5]
- *Other unexplained physical ailments*
- *Medical needs remaining unmet*

## Signs of Emotional Abuse

Sometimes parents are not aware of what can be emotionally harmful to their child. It's helpful for caregivers, family members, and friends to know what constitutes emotional abuse. Some behaviors of abusive parents include:

- *Bullying, shaming, or humiliating a child*
- *Calling a child names and making them feel less-than*
- *Telling a child they're "no good," "worthless," "bad," or "a mistake"*
- *Yelling at or threatening a child*
- *Giving a child the silent treatment*
- *Withholding physical affection from a child*
- *Exposing the child to violence* [6]

## Signs of Neglect

Sometimes a parent isn't actively abusing the child, but they are

5. Ibid
6. "Child Abuse and Neglect" HelpGuide. Accessed April 1, 2021. https://www. helpguide.org/articles/abuse/child-abuse-and-neglect.htm

still unable to meet the child's needs. A parent who is abusing alcohol or drugs, for example, may not be mentally and emotionally competent enough to care for their child. [7]

It took a lot of work for me to recover from the trauma I experienced, which is why I think it's important for people to realize that child abuse has harmful lasting effects which can be mitigated by the right kinds of intervention.

## Short- and Long-Term Effects of Child Abuse

Immediate and obvious effects of physically abuse include marks on the child's body. These might be broken bones, bruises, cuts, or the development of shaken baby syndrome (for children one year old and under). Some of these can lead to more severe physical disabilities, such as brain damage, learning disabilities, or cerebral palsy.

The long term effects of child abuse can be more difficult to measure and might be overlooked by others once the child is placed in a safer environment.

Long-term stress can inhibit healthy growth in the body and the brain and lead to an array of health issues such as diabetes, lung disease, malnutrition, vision problems, a heart attack, back problems, high blood pressure, migraine headaches, chronic pulmonary problems, bowel disease, chronic fatigue, a stroke, or even cancer. Research has shown that child abuse and neglect can turn on certain genes in the child that make them more susceptible to these conditions.

Child abuse and neglect can inhibit proper brain growth and formation as well. The child's brain may be smaller than others or have abnormalities in certain areas. They may develop difficulties in their amygdala, for example, making it difficult to process their emotions. This can lead to issues with self-regulation. They could also have inhibited growth in their hippocampus, leading to learning disabilities and memory problems later in life.  A

7. Ibid

vast number of other important parts of the brain could be affected or underdeveloped, leading to many different obstacles for the child to function in healthy ways. However, with proper interventions, there is evidence that these children can recover what they've lost. [8]

However, the physical outcomes are often not the most severe or lasting effects. Most of the time, it is the emotional and psychological trauma the child has endured which poses the greatest threat. This can have many negative short term outcomes for the child, including a feeling of isolation from others, being fearful of others and having difficulty trusting and connecting with others. These children may act out to get attention or they may withdraw and not tell anyone that something is wrong. [9]

In recent years, society has become more aware of the importance of our emotional and psychological health. Child abuse and can have long-lasting effects on both of these things. Child abuse and neglect can lead to long term cognitive difficulties and overall poor mental health. Abused children have increased risk for developing depression and anxiety, and making suicide attempts.[10] I developed anxiety from the abusive environment I grew up in, and it has stuck with me to this day. It still inhibits me from leading the kind of life I want to.

There are also several severe long term psychological conditions that can be caused by childhood abuse and neglect. One of these is post-traumatic stress disorder, which can make the person feel stuck, like they are continually re-experiencing the traumatic abuse. They may start avoiding anything that brings up these difficult feelings and psychological experiences. They might feel shame and fear often and have a heightened startle

8. Long-Term Consequences of Child Abuse and Neglect. Child Welfare Information Gateway. Factsheet. April 2019. Accessed February 10, 2021. https://www.childwelfare.gov/pubPDFs/long_term_consequences.pdf
9. Ibid.
10. Ibid.

reflex. They can be irritable and moody, and might spend a lot of their time scanning their surroundings for signs of danger. This could lead to the abuse of substances to try to cope or becoming defiant and argumentative towards others.[11]

Along with the physical and psychological outcomes, child abuse and neglect can have negative behavioral effects. Children who are abused are more likely to become delinquent and mixed up in criminal activity. They can develop antisocial behaviors and then bond with other children who have the same tendencies. Studies have shown that this is much more common in boys, who externalize their negative feelings, versus girls, who are more likely to internalize their feelings.[12] However, both genders are susceptible to delinquency, teen pregnancy, low academic performance, and drug use.[13] As adolescents and teenagers, these children will be more likely to pass on the mistreatment to others, preying on younger children and treating them the same way they were treated.[14]

This doesn't have to be the case, however. I think these children can be helped and set on the right track. I am starting a program to help at-risk youth which will help these kids build self-confidence and succeed in life. It will be a hands-on "big brother" type of program that will teach kids about real-life issues and solutions. I want these kids to learn how to handle life and to give them opportunities to try new things or learn more about the things they love.

I want them to learn that it's okay to fail at something and to provide a safe space where they can experience unconditional love and support. I want to provide mental health workshops to

11. Ibid.
12. Ibid.
13. "Effects of Abuse." Butterfly Bridge Children's Advocacy Center. Accessed February 10, 2021. http://www.butterflybridgecac.org/resourcesabuseeffects.php
14. Long-Term Consequences of Child Abuse and Neglect. Child Welfare Information Gateway. Factsheet. April 2019. Accessed February 10, 2021. https://www.childwelfare.gov/pubPDFs/long_term_consequences.pdf

help them to work through their emotional issues, too.

I envision my organization to be a place that will empower these youths to join the workforce and believe in their abilities. It will teach them how to build their resumes and help them get started in their careers. Through sports, activities, and hobbies, my organization will help at-risk kids be more social, brave, and confident.

Learning about trauma and its effects is only the first step. To heal, I've had to learn how to process things and have gone to counseling. Counseling helped to open my eyes to some of the symptoms caused by my trauma and to learn healthy coping strategies.

Success doesn't happen overnight, especially if you've been through trauma. Starting a career and pursuing your dreams while you're dealing with anxiety and working through your past are difficult. Some days it feels like one step forward and two steps back. However, I can look back and see many accomplishments in my life. I am proud of what I've achieved, especially considering my past.

# CHAPTER 9:
# THE JOURNEY FORWARD

The scars and trauma of my past are no longer the canvas I paint from—they are the canvas I paint over every day in my pursuit to create something far more beautiful.

## Responding to Stress and Triggers

I never slowed down enough to think about why I felt so stressed and anxious all the time. My family has been my main motivation to realize when I'm being triggered and not react.

My wife and I have had a rocky relationship from the start. Part of this is because I wasn't aware of why I was feeling certain things and reacting by lashing out at her. I didn't know why I always felt anxious and miserable around my family, and I always thought they were the cause. Because of this, my wife and I were on and off for a while, and the last time we separated, it was for two years. I thought she was making me miserable.

Growing up, Ray acted like I was bothering him if I tried to talk to him about anything. He had a "what do you want now?" type of attitude, and I became afraid to talk to him. As an adult, I've realized that I was acting the same way toward my daughter and that she was afraid to talk to me. Part of the reason I separated from my wife was my not wanting to act angry around my kids.

The initial reason I started going to therapy was because I noticed that I was feeling a lot of anger toward my daughter. I didn't know how to handle my intense feelings of anger and anxiety, and I didn't want them to hurt the people I loved with these emotions.

Before I started therapy, I was angry at my daughter and I hated my wife. Therapy helped me to identify that I had anxiety, and I realized that I was actually very happy with my wife. My family wasn't the problem—it was everything I had been through in the past, which I now realized the significance of.

My wife and I have been back together since September 2020. Even though we were living in separate households, we both wanted to see the kids, so we quarantined together. We were able to work things out, and I've been doing a lot of personal work since then, trying to work through my struggles and become a better person.

My family and I have been working on identifying each other's anxieties and being more patient with each other. We try to talk about our feelings and be sensitive to each other's struggles. The open communication has been very helpful and healing.

Growing up, we never talked about our feelings in my family. There was no patience extended to each other. Everyone simply reacted to one another by lashing out or withdrawing. With my own family as an adult, I'm turning over a new leaf. We're revealing a lot of ourselves to each other.

I met my wife in 2009, a month before my father passed. We've been married since 2013, but we didn't share with each other on a deep level like we do now. I've realized that I wasn't open with her about a lot of things because it made me think about my upbringing and the things about it I didn't want to remember.

Even though my wife knows about some of my childhood, there are many memories I've never shared with anyone, including her. I've been trying to be more open with her and share why I am the way that I am and why I feel the things that I feel.

Every day, I still battle the urge to snap for no reason. I don't have a lot of quiet time right now. It's hard to get alone time, and my family and I have been triggering each other's anxiety sometimes. , but I'm happy that we've made progress as a family and that these struggles have brought us closer together.

## People Who Have Helped Me Heal

My wife has been instrumental to my healing. She's always

pushed me to be better and has tried to help me identify my problems. Without her continuous support, I wouldn't feel like I'm on the right path and progressing. Together, we have grown so much, and without her, I don't know if I would be where I am. It takes a strong woman to deal with some of my past transgressions and faults. However, she continuously gives me her unconditional love and reminds me that life is worth it and having love is vital.

My kids have also been instrumental in my recovery, and they're the reason I push myself hard every day. I want to over-come my anger and anxiety because I don't want to pass it on to them. I don't want them to have the childhood I did, and I don't want to treat them the way I was treated. Being a father of three is no walk in the park, but it is worth it. My children's love has pulled me out of some dark places, and when I look at them, I am reminded that doing better isn't optional. I owe it to my children to do better because they deserve the absolute best version of me. One thing I never realized as a kid was that my parents were also trying to figure out how to navigate life. As children, we have this notion that our parents have it all together and know everything, but that is far from the truth. When my children look back, I hope they see that my wife and I did our absolute best to figure out what life meant, and that we gave them our 100% at all times.

## Steps I'm Taking to Heal

In September 2019, I started seeing a therapist. My wife had been begging me to see one for years, but I never wanted to. I didn't feel ready. Before she and I separated for the last time, she asked me again. I decided it was finally time, so I started seeing my therapist, Jeremy.

I've been going to counseling for a year and a half now, and it has opened my eyes to so many things about myself, my emotions, and my past. Unfortunately, I stopped working during the pandemic and lost my health insurance, so I couldn't see him for six months.

In therapy, I was able to change some of my negative behaviors toward my family by becoming more mindful. When I'm with my family now, I try to be present. I have to get out of my head and be respectful of my time with them. I try to listen and focus on them and not think about other things when I'm spending time with my family.

When I started going to counseling again, it helped me to face my anxiety and depression. I recently started doing Eye Movement Desensitization and Reprocessing therapy, a type of therapy designed to work through trauma.

I've been working on finding my safe space, a place in my mind where I can feel peaceful. This is important for EMDR since I'm revisiting traumatic and difficult memories. Going back into these memories can trigger anxiety and depression, the very things I'm trying to work on. Focusing on my safe space helps.

With my EMDR specialist, I realized that as a child, I was often alone. Since none of my siblings lived with me, I grew up like an only child . I had a lot of quiet time and a nice, big backyard. No one else was around, and we had a forest preserve near my house where I could explore by myself.

My peaceful place is from my experience as a child, going to the forest preserve near Ray and Rochelle's house. I would go to the forest preserve to relax. I would walk along the trail on the river, and if I walked far enough, I would go and find a fallen tree and sit by myself. Lake Michigan was close by, and when I got to the lake, I would look out at the water and feel myself calm down.

When I feel my anxiety kicking in today, I go back to this place in my mind. I can still smell the lake and hear the waves crashing against the shore. It was my own special place where I reminded myself that I would overcome. And I will overcome. We *will* all overcome.

# APPENDIX:
# HELP FOR THOSE DEALING WITH ABUSE

If you know of a child who has been abused, Children's Advocacy Centers (CACs) can be a big help. These centers have child protection staff who are familiar with the laws and procedures that protect children from abuse. They are connected with law enforcement and can help to take legal action on a child's behalf. They have family advocates who are skilled in helping children find the support and care they need, as well as medical and mental health professionals who help children who have faced trauma, abuse, or neglect.

Every year, the CACs serve over 370,000 children who have been abused. These centers also work to prevent abuse by educating over two million people every year.[15]

**Chicago Children's Advocacy Center website:**
https://www.chicagocac.org/

In the New York Times bestseller, *The Body Keeps the Score*, Bessel Van Der Kolk, M.D. talks about the road to healing the body and mind from trauma. He talks about the idea of owning yourself. Someone who has experienced trauma will inevitably face issues with their limbic system, which is responsible for the fight-or-flight feelings you experience. You will either be in a state of hyperarousal, which can cause anxiety and angry outbursts, or you may shut down and sink into a state of depression. To combat this, there are several physical and mental steps that we can take:

1. **Practice deep breathing.** This can help you calm your body and get out of this reactive state.

2. **Practice mindfulness.** Mindfulness is self-awareness about

---

15 . https://www.nationalchildrensalliance.org/media-room/national-statistics-on-child-abuse/

what is currently happening in your body and with your emotions. Taking a minute to notice if your body is tense or if your mind is racing can help you to explore possible solutions for taking care of yourself and can give you back the power of choice. You'll also want to notice the interplay between your thoughts, emotions, and physical sensations. People who have experienced trauma tend to want to tune out what they are feeling, but tuning in can be educational and empowering.

3. **Form relationships with people who will support you.** Since trauma often involves feeling unsafe and having your trust broken, it is important to feel safe and learn to rebuild trust with others. Find loving and supportive people who will not treat you the same way that those who abused you did.

4. **Find a professional therapist.** When you look for a therapist, you need to find one that you feel comfortable and safe with who will help you to face and heal from your trauma. There are many different techniques therapists might use to help you heal. These could include prescribing medication, EMDR, self-regulation, talk therapy, teaching you about self-leadership, and neurofeedback.

**EMDR** stands for Eye Movement Desensitization and Reprocessing. It is performed by alternately activating each side of the brain by moving a finger or object back and forth in front of a person, alternately blinking dots on either side of the person's face, or placing pulsers in the person's hands which alternate back and forth. Then, the person is asked to go back in their mind to the traumatic incident and to notice what they are feeling and experiencing.

The goal of EMDR is to help the person undergoing treatment understand their experience and place it in the past. One of the symptoms of PTSD is the constant reliving of trauma. Recalling the traumatic memory in its context in the past and processing the things that you were feeling and thinking that you weren't paying attention to in the moment helps the brain to put the incidents in their proper place so that it feels like something that happened in the past instead of intruding on the present.

**Self-regulation** has to do with the nervous system, which trauma and PTSD can negatively affect. There is a calming part of our nervous system (parasympathetic) and a fight-or-flight part of our nervous system (sympathetic). Those suffering from PTSD and symptoms of trauma need to learn how to activate and turn off both systems. This is called regulation. One effective strategy to learn how to do this is through exercise and yoga.

**Talk therapy**, or psychotherapy, is when a patient talks through the problems they are facing, and the therapist listens and tries to help the person find solutions through making behavioral changes, understanding themselves and their relationships more, talking through painful memories, building self-esteem, and exploring other options such as play therapy or art therapy. [16]

**Self-leadership** occurs when a person recovers their confident, calm, and curious self that has been buried underneath the trauma and negative coping mechanisms they developed as a result. This self can help them understand different parts of themselves that have formed over time and help those parts heal.

**Neurofeedback** is about understanding how the brain processes events and experiences and using that information to try to process things differently. The patient is taught to slow down certain processes and boost others in order to use better judgment and become less reactive. This can be done through electroencephalograms (EEGs), electrodes, or computer-generated feedback. Trauma and PTSD change brainwaves, and it can take some time for a person to learn how to normalize them again. [17]

16. https://www.psychiatry.org/patients-families/psychotherapy
17. Ibid.

CPSIA information can be obtained
at www.ICGtesting.com
Printed in the USA
BVHW072207040423
661733BV00012B/355

9 781666 400311